THE GOSPEL OF
JOHN
STUDY HELPS

By
Kurt Kennedy, M(BS), D.Min.

All scripture references are from the King James Bible

Requests for copies or information should be addressed to:
kennedykt@yahoo.com

ISBN: 978-0692389379

True Word Press

ACKNOWLEDGEMENTS

I would like to offer much thanks to John Knowles for the countless hours he spent proofreading this pamphlet, to my wife Wendy for the layout and graphic design, and to my Sunday School classes for following me through this study of John's Gospel.

INTRODUCTION

The gospel of John is one of the greatest arguments in the entire Bible for the Deity of Jesus Christ. If one needs to be persuaded of the Deity of Jesus Christ they only need to read through this great gospel record. John tells us that he wrote this account for this express purpose:

But these are written, that ye might believe that Jesus is the Christ, the Son of God; and that believing ye might have life through his name. (John 20:31)

While each gospel account focuses on different aspects of our Lord's ministry and personage, it is John that shows us God manifest in the flesh. This is overwhelmingly shown on every page. It is John that brings us the great "I AM" aspects of Christ. I am the Vine, the Branch, the Door, the Good Shepherd and the Resurrection and the Life. John also gives us the symbols of Christ's deity. Jesus is the water of life, bread from heaven, the serpent lifted up and the very Lamb of God. And while all that is contained in John's gospel should be proof enough that God visited this earth in the person of Jesus Christ, John adds the following:

And there are also many other things which Jesus did, the which, if they should be written every one, I suppose that even the world itself could not contain the books that should be written. Amen. (John 21:25)

There is one other truth that John brings forth throughout this gospel account, and that is belief in Jesus Christ is eternal life. From the very outset of this book to the very last page, belief in Christ for eternal life is the issue:

But as many as received him, to them gave he power to

become the sons of God, even to them that believe on his name: (John 1:12)

But these are written, that ye might believe that Jesus is the Christ, the Son of God; and that believing ye might have life through his name. (John 20:31)

It is therefore the desire of John that as you read and study this gospel record that you see Jesus Christ for who He is, the Son of the living God.

CHAPTER 1

In the Beginning was the Word
- Why the Word? Because God is showing that He is going to manifest Himself not only in flesh, (John 1:14) but also through the spoken word. (John 6:63,68;Ps. 19; I Peter 1:23)
- This is why the attack on what God hath spoken. (Mark 4:15)
- Thus the Bible used by the Jehovah's Witness the New World Translation reads "the word was a god"
- When our Lord comes back He bares this title (Rev. 19:13)
- Thus He is the Alpha and Omega (Rev. 1:8,17)
- See I John 5:7

The Word was God
- The Scriptures plainly teach that Jesus Christ is God, Christ being the express image of God, for the Word became flesh and dwelt among us. (John 1:14; Col. 1:15; Heb. 1:3)
- Jesus Christ claimed to be God (John 8:58; 10:30; 14:9)
- Scripture plainly declares¬ He is Immanuel, God with us. (Matt. 1:23 cf. Isa. 7:14 cf. I Tim. 3:16)

The Word was with God
- Before the foundation of the world (John 17:5, 24; cf. Prov. 8:22-31)

All things made by Him
- Col. 1:16-17
- Gen. 1:26
- Thus, the God breather (Ps. 33:6) became the sin bearer (II Cor. 5:21)

7

In Him was Life
- God is eternal life and this life He giveth to the Son (John 5:26 cf. John 17:1-3)
- The Son giveth it to those that believeth in Him (John 3:16; John 6:40)
- Man lost this life (I Cor. 15:21), but Christ restored life to a fallen world (I Cor. 15:22; Rom. 5:12-19)

In Him was Light
- God is Light (I John 1:1:5)
- Thus, Christ is Light (John 8:12)
- All light emanates from God the Father (I Tim 6:16), whether it be the:
  - Light of creation (Rev. 21:23; Gen. 1:3)
  - Light of knowledge (2 Cor. 5:6)
  - Light of scripture (Ps. 119:105)
  - Light of thought (Ps. 18:28

Life is the Light of Men
- When someone hears the gospel they receive light! (2 Cor. 4:4-6)
- The expression: "The lights are turned on"
  - Paul had scales fall from his eyes (Acts 9:18)
  - The man possessed with a devil when healed clothed and in his right mind (Matt.   5:15)
  - This is why one needs to be saved first before He/she can see or understand spiritual things.
- Once you're saved you are called to:
  - Walk as children of light (Eph. 5:8)
  - Put on the armour of light (Rom. 13:12)
  - And are partakers with others of the children of light (Col. 1:12)

The Ministry of John the Baptist (vss. 15-27)
- Sent from God (John 1:6 see Luke 1:11-17)

- Son of Zacharias and Elizabeth
- Miraculous Birth (Luke 1:7-13)
- Filled with the Holy Ghost from his mother's womb (Luke 1:41)

John's twofold ministry:
- FIRST– He would herald the kingdom "at hand"
  - It was prophesied that a "forerunner" would come to prepare the way for the King, prior to the final week of Daniel's time schedule ticking off and the King coming back. (Mal. 3:1 cf. Isaiah 40:3)
  - John had the privilege of not merely proclaiming the reality of the kingdom but would be the one who would proclaim the "kingdom at hand" (Matt. 3:2)
  - This made John the greatest of the Old Testament prophets (Matt. 11:9-13 cf. Luke 16:16)
- SECOND– He would confront the nation for their sinfulness in walking contrary to God's path, in order to turn the people to the Father, thereby avoiding the coming Day of Wrath, (Isa. 40:1-3) and offer to them the prescription of cleansing.

The confusion over john's ministry (1:21-22):
- The Pharisees sent Priests and Levites to ask is John Elijah or that Prophet (Deut. 18:32)?
- The confusion over this issue is due to the Pharisees false interpretation of Malachi 3:1 and Malachi 4:5.

The close of John's ministry is seen in Matthew 4:12,17 and John 3:30.

Baptism of Christ (vss. 28-51)
(John 1:28-34 cf. Matt. 3:13-17)
The purpose:

* To make manifest to Israel (31). This was the purpose of John's ministry, thus his joy is full (John 3:29,30)
* To fulfill all righteousness (Matt. 3:13-17)
* He became sin for us (2 Cor. 5:21)
* He was made a curse for us (Gal. 3:13, 4:4,5)
* Numbered with the transgressors (Isa. 53)
• The Spirit from God & the voice from heaven (John 1:32 cf. Matt. 3:16,17)
• This had not happened to those who had been baptized, hence "lo, the heavens were opened" Matt. 3:16. All this was to make Him manifest to Israel. Notice all members of the Godhead are present.

The Lamb of God (vss. 29,36)
• He is the fulfillment of the type of the lamb throughout the sacrificial system, He is the Passover Lamb. (Ex. 12:5; I Pt. 1:18,19; I Cor. 5:7)

Christ's Remnant of Believers (vss. 35-51)
• Andrew and John (1:35-39)
• Peter (Andrew's brother 1:40-42)
• Philip (1:43)
• Nathanael (1:44-51)
* Verse 51—This is in response to Nathanael responding "thou art the King of Israel" cf. Gen. 28:12

CHAPTER 2

Marriage of Cana (vss. 1-11)

- The Time- (2:1) The 3rd day following the last day listed. Day 1 (19-28); Day 2 (29-34); Day 3 (35-42); Day 4 (43-51). Thus making it the 7th day that this miracle takes place.
- The Type- My hour has not yet come (2:4)
  *The 7th pictures that millennial rest (Matt. 26:29 cf. Luke 22:18,30)
- The Purpose of the Miracle (2:11)
  *Manifest His glory, thus they believed on Him (11)

Cleansing of the Temple (vss. 13-22)

- The Timing—"the Jews' Passover" (vs. 13) Thus the reason for all the animals of sacrifice, and the changers of money would be because of all the Gentile proselytes.

- The House—Make not my Father's house an house of merchandise (vs. 16)
  *At this time it is still His Father's House but at the final pronouncement against   Israel our Lord will declare "your house is left unto you desolate" (Matt. 23:38,39)

- The Temple—"Destroy this temple and in three days I will raise it up" (vs. 19)
  * Once again not understanding spiritual things (Matt. 15:1-20; Matt. 16:5-12)
  *This was used against our Lord to lay false charges against Him (Matt. 26:60,61)
  *Our Lord was mocked on the cross concerning this statement (Matt. 27:39,40)

11

The Belief of the Crowd (vss. 23-25)

* Many believed for the miracle's sake, but our Lord did not commit Himself unto them for He knew what was in man. (Example: Matt. 9:3-4 also Judas John 6:64, 70-71)

CHAPTER 3

The Purpose of the Epistle (vss. 1-21)

This chapter further illustrates the truth presented in chapter 2:23-25. Many believe in His name, i.e. "we know thou art a teacher come from God.." (3:2) but they do not believe as Peter did (Matthew 16:16). Thus, John wrote and recorded the Epistle for this very purpose, that people might believe that Jesus is the Christ, the Son of God, and believing they might have life through His name. (John 20:31)

Nicodemus may have held more than one office and title, but he has passed into the Scriptures with but one title, and will be known for all time as the Pharisee that "came to Jesus by night." (John 3:2; 7:50; 19:39)

• The New Birth: Nicodemus was not "born of God" (3:5,7) though he thought he and his kind were begotten of God because they were descendants of Abraham (Notice "we" of 3:2 and John 8:33,39). Nicodemus is genuinely confused in the matter (vss. 4, 7, 9) Nicodemus was as the bulk of Israel who also sought righteousness by the law (Luke 18:18-27 cf. Rom. 9:30-33 See also John 9:34).

• The need for birth: Physical birth and spiritual birth: One must be born of flesh (being born of water) and Spirit (being born again of God) (3:4-8). Just as wind blows and no man can see it, so is everyone that is born of God.

• How is one born of God?: Nicodemus asks, "How can these things be?" (vs. 9) Answer- believe and be saved, look and live! Just as they beheld the serpent in the wilderness and they were healed (vs. 14 cf. Num. 21:9), those who believe when the Son of God is lifted up get eternal life (vs. 15).

• The Reproving light of God (vss. 19-21) It is not the evil deeds that sinners do that damn them, but those sins are what prevent them from coming to the light; "...men loved darkness rather than light." Thus, Nicodemus came at night.

The Ministry of John the Baptist (vss. 22-36)

Questions arise from John the Baptist's disciples (3:25-26), and in the following verses John reminds them of his testimony "beyond Jordan," how he clearly stated he was not the Christ but rather was sent before Him (i.e. the forerunner). John is transferring his ministry to the Lord's ministry, and therefore if these followers are going to continue in their understanding, they need to transfer their submission to the Lord and His authority. Notice in Matthew 9:14-17 there are those who are in the dark as to the Lord's ministry. They had not had the benefit other kingdom believers had in following the Lord and continuing in the things He taught up to this point. Also notice that the religious leaders did not even take the first step in submitting to John the Baptist's ministry (Luke 7:29-30; Matt. 21:23-27).

• He must increase but I must decrease: It is at this time that John the Baptist will begin to "decrease" his ministry (30) and though his "joy is fulfilled" (29) his ministry will not come to an end until he is cast into prison (24). It is at that time that Jesus' ministry begins (Matthew 4:12 cf. vs. 17) thus all submission should have been transferred to the Lord at this point. However some did not (See Acts 18:24-26).

14

• He that hath received his testimony hath set to his seal that God is true: Again this is the benefit for those who transfer their submission from following John the Baptist to our Lord's ministry: they will grow in knowledge of the truth. They will have the benefit of further education (i.e. the sermon on the mount). Notice John 15:8-27; transferring from John the Baptist to the Lord's Ministry is a prequalification for being one of the Twelve (cf. Acts 1:22).

• All things into His hand: All things from God the Father are committed unto God the Son until the fullness of times. When the Son hath put down all rule and authority, He Himself will become subject unto the Father (I Corinthian 15:24,28).

CHAPTER 4

The people termed "Samaritans" were a mixed race of people. They came about upon the captivity of the Northern tribes of Israel by the Assyrians (King Shalmaneser) at which time most of Israel was deported out of the land into regions within the Assyrian empire (2 Kings 17:1-23). It was at this time that the Assyrians imported foreigners into the land of Samaria who inter-married with the remaining Israelites (2 Kings 17:24).

The Mountain and Place of worship: When the foreigners were brought into the land of Samaria (2 Kings 17:24) God brought lions upon them to slay them (2 Kings 17:25). In response to this the Assyrians brought in priests from the deported Israelites who set up false worship in Mount Gerizim (2 Kings 17:25-28).

The stigma associated with the Samaritans: Because the Samaritans were a mixed race of people they were ostracized by the Jews. Under Zerubbabel they were rejected from helping rebuild the temple, and tried to prevent the work both under Ezra and Nehemiah (Ezra 4:1-10 cf. Nehemiah 4:1-2). (See John 8:48)

The Samaritan Woman (vss. 1-26)
• *Spiritual not Physical (11):* Once again the individual people that our Lord deals with are looking at the physical instead of the spiritual truth (Nicodemus and the new birth (3:4); the woman at the well and living water (4:10-14); disciples and meat (4:31-34). (See: John 6:54-56)

• *Her Request and His Response (7-15):* Notice that she desires this "living water" and therefore our Lord goes to the first step in receiving "living water" i.e. everlasting life: she's a sinner! (16-19)

• *Worship (19-24):* The question of where to worship is brought up. Worship prior to our Lord's revealing all truth was according to types and shadows , thus law came by Moses but grace and truth came by Jesus Christ. Jesus Christ is the one that will fulfill all the types and shadows of the law, so now they that worship Him must worship in "Spirit and Truth." Notice verses 25,26.

The Disciples (vss. 31-38)

• *Disciples Return:* Upon the woman at the well "leaving her water pots" (28) telling her town to "come see a man which told me all things that ever I did," the disciples return from getting meat (vs. 8).

• *Disciples' Reaction:* "Master eat" (31). Our Lord replies that He has "meat to eat that ye know not of" (32). The disciples once again are confused over this matter, only looking at the physical meat (33).

• *The Lord's Meat:* The Lord was teaching that the meat they need to be concerned with is "to do the work of Him that sent me" (34). This is what the disciples need to be occupied with, and in so doing, the Lord will provide for their physical needs (See Matt. 6:25-34).

• *Harvest:* Our Lord teaches the disciples that they are to be about the Father's business, and thus teaches a further truth. Jesus looks unto the fields that are four months to harvest (35) and says, "Say not ye, There are yet four months, and then cometh harvest?" Then He turns and sees the crowd of Samaritans streaming down the road, coming from their hometown (40) to see the man that told the woman everything she ever did. Jesus then says unto His disciples, "behold, I say unto you, Lift up your eyes, and look on the fields; for they are white already to harvest." Here comes a harvest that is ripe for the picking!

• *Sowing and Reaping:* Our Lord takes this opportunity to teach the great doctrinal truth that whether one sows or reaps, all will "rejoice together" (36-38). (See I Corinthians 3:1-9)

The Samaritans (vss. 39-42)
Notice again that it is the Samaritans that believe on Christ, while the Jews of Jerusalem continue to reject (John 7:45-48). Because of the woman's testimony the Samaritans, "know that indeed this is the Christ, the Saviour of the world" (42).

The Nobleman's Son (vss. 43-54)
• *His Request:* Jesus travels to Cana of Galilee where He turned water into wine (46). A Nobleman travels from Capernaum where his son is sick unto death (47). The Nobleman makes a request to have Jesus come down and heal his son (47).

• *Jesus' Response:* The Lord, seeing all those who believed merely for the miracles' sake (John 2:23-25; 3:2), responds with, "Except ye see signs and wonders, ye will not believe." Our Lord harkens to the persistent cries of the Nobleman saying, "Go thy way; thy son liveth."

• *Belief and Assurance:* "And the man believed the word that Jesus had spoken unto him, and he went his way." The Nobleman, returning home, meets up with his servants who inform him his son lives (51), and upon inquiring what time it was that his son recovered, comes to the realization that it was the same hour that Jesus said unto him, "thy son liveth." Belief precedes assurance, for the Nobleman "knew."

CHAPTER 5

An Angel and the Pool (vss. 1-4)
Some facts: 1. An Angel comes down at a "certain season." 2. Only the first person to "step" into the pool was made whole, no one else, even though there was a "great multitude." Thus it was the luck of the draw as to who made it into the pool for healing. 3. This pool was in the walls of Jerusalem by the sheep gate. Jerusalem was totally apostate at the time of our Lord's ministry. The religious leaders were of their father the devil (8:44) and our Lord had already attempted to cleanse the temple in John chapter three. 4. It would seem the angel and the "troubling of the water" was keeping the multitude bound to the temple. 5. This story of the pool follows the account of our Lord dealing with the woman at the well, wherein He offered "living water" (4:14) that "whosoever" drinketh shall never thirst again.

Healing of the Impotent Man (vss. 5-9)
This healing is instantaneous, "and immediately the man was made whole" (9). This was done on the Sabbath day (9), which becomes the source of contention for the religious leaders: first he was healed on the Sabbath (16) and second he was carrying his bed (10).

Religious Leaders' Response (vss. 15-18)
Once the religious leaders found out who it was that healed the impotent man and told him to take his bed and walk, "therefore did the Jews persecute Jesus, and sought to slay him" (16).

Our Lord's response (17-30)
"My Father worketh hitherto, and I work" (17). Because of this statement the Jews "sought the more to kill him" for He made Himself equal with God" (18). Our Lord deals

with the issue of healing on the Sabbath in John 7:19-24. Just as the Father works on the Sabbath so the Son works. The Sabbath was made for man because, in a fallen state, man will not have mercy; he will toil and work himself into the ground, even to death! Thus our Lord's statement, "I will have mercy and not sacrifice" (Matt. 12:7) and "The sabbath was made for man, and not man for the Sabbath" (Mark 2:27). Think about it, if God were to withdraw His hand for a single moment creation would cease to exist. Our breath is in His hand (Dan. 5:23), He upholds all things by the word of His power (Heb.1:3), by Him all things consist (Col. 1:17). Do we not breathe on the Sabbath day? Does the whole of creation labor, grow, or decompose? Life; death; do these stand still on the Sabbath day? "My Father worketh hitherto, and I work"

What follows in verses 20-30 is our Lord responding to the religious leaders "marveling" over the "rising of the impotent man." If they "marvel" over this, wait until Christ raises the dead (28-30). Now, all things are given to the Son; life was given Him, thus He is able to raise the dead. He is the salvation of them that believe and therefore all judgment is also committed into His hands: For as the Father hath life in himself; so hath he given to the Son to have life in himself; And hath given him authority to execute judgment also, because he is the Son of man. John 5:26-27
>   *The dead hearing His voice (Eph. 4:9 cf. I Pt. 3:19)
>   *The raising of the dead fulfilled in (Matthew 27:52)
>   *The judgment of all (II Corinthians 5:9,10 cf. Phil. 2:10)

Bearing Witness (vss. 32-47)

Jesus, being the Son of God and the only way unto the Father, and having all things committed into His hands, is

the source of all the contention. In verse 30 He states:
I can of mine own self do nothing: as I hear, I judge: and my judgment is just; because I seek not mine own will, but the will of the Father which hath sent me. (John 5:30)

In what follows our Lord is going to bring in four witnesses that testify to this fact: John the Baptist (33-35), the works of Christ (36), the Father (37) and the Scriptures (39).
"That in the mouth of two or three witnesses every word may be established." (Matthew 18:16)

• John the Baptist (32-35): John was called forth to be "a burning and shining light," John bore testimony that he was not "the Light" but "a light" (1:6-9). John was only a voice; Jesus Christ is the "Word." On two occasions John testified that Jesus was the Lamb of God (1:29,36).

• THE WORKS OF CHRIST (VS. 36)
When John started to doubt the Lord's ministry, Jesus told John's disciples of the works He'd done, and those works witnessed for Him: Then Jesus answering said unto them, Go your way, and tell John what things ye have seen and heard; how that the blind see, the lame walk, the lepers are cleansed, the deaf hear, the dead are raised, to the poor the gospel is preached. (Luke 7:22)

The 'works" were to be the evidence that He had been sent of the Father: If I do not the works of my Father, believe me not. But if I do, though ye believe not me, believe the works: that ye may know, and believe, that the Father is in me, and I in him. (John 10:37-38)

These works are the "power of the world to come" (Heb. 6:5)

• THE FATHER (VS. 37)

The Father bore witness to Him, and all the multitude around saw: And Jesus, when he was baptized, went up straightway out of the water: and, lo, the heavens were opened unto him, and he saw the Spirit of God descending like a dove, and lighting upon him: And lo a voice from heaven, saying, This is my beloved Son, in whom I am well pleased. (Matthew 3:16-17)

The Father bore witness to Him again at the mount of Transfiguration. A bright cloud overshadowed them: ...And behold a voice out of the cloud, which said, This is my beloved Son, in whom I am well pleased; hear ye him. (Matthew 17:5)

• THE SCRIPTURES (VS. 39)

This last witness is the one that remains with us, the Scriptures: Then said he, Lo, I come to do thy will, O God. He taketh away the first, that he may establish the second. (Hebrews 10:9)

They were told to search the Scriptures, in contrast to their vain commandments of men that only make the word of God void. Specifically they were to look into Moses' scriptures, and if they believed them they would believe on Him, for Moses wrote of Jesus (45-47). Their problem was they sought honor one from another, rather than letting the Scriptures interpret themselves (44).

The implication in these last verses is clear, if they "trust in Moses" then they should "trust in Him" for Moses wrote of Him!

CHAPTER 6

The Feeding of the Five Thousand (vss. 1-14)
The feeding of the five thousand is recorded by all of the gospels (Matt. 14; Mark 6 and Luke 9). The event foreshadows a future time in which the believing remnant of Israel will be fed in the wilderness as they flee persecution from the Anti-christ and his army. When considering this account one must look at the whole of the chapter in order to gain appreciation of the truth being taught.

• *Context to consider:* The feeding of the five thousand was for the benefit of the disciples, to "prove them" (3-9). Secondly, the feeding of the five thousand was for the multitude that followed, to teach them of their need to receive Him (26-51) that they might have everlasting life (27,40,47,51), in contrast to the bread in the wilderness which those who ate thereof died (49).

• *Education for the disciples:* This event occurred in a desert place (Matt. 14:15) and seeing a "great company come" the disciples ask "Whence shall we buy bread that these may eat?" (5) This question was to prove the disciples (6) and the event would be for their benefit.

• *The teaching:* This event is tied to the giving of manna to the Israelites in the wilderness under Moses (31,32,49 cf. Ps. 78:19-25). The disciples need to understand that God is able to furnish a table for them in the wilderness; they are not to doubt the provision of the Lord as did those who "ate manna in the wilderness and perished." When our Lord was tempted, the Devil said, "If thou be the Son of God, command this stone that it be made bread" (Luke 4:3). Our Lord responded by saying, "Man shall not live by bread alone but by every word of God." Thus, the disciples needed to trust in what God had promised He would do for them, over their seemingly hopeless situation. Did not God call them? Did not God tell them He would provide for them?

• *A prophetic glimpse:* The feeding of the five thousand looks forward to the day in which the Lord will provide sustenance for His remnant during the Tribulation as they flee the Anti-christ and his armies (Matt. 24:15,16; Hosea 2:14; Revelation 12:6,14).

• *Education for the multitude:* The event of the feeding of the five thousand was also for the benefit of the "great multitude." (2) Our Lord now uses the event to teach the crowd of their need to receive or partake of Him if they are going to have everlasting life. (26-51). Our Lord and the great multitude have a lengthy discourse concerning who He is (27-65) which will end with many of His disciples going back and "walking no more with Him." (66)

The Bread from Heaven (vss. 26-51)
The overall thought throughout this discourse is regarding the bread that was provided at the feeding of the five thousand (26), the manna that was provided in the wilderness (31,49) and the true Bread from heaven, Jesus Christ Himself (32-35, 47-51).

Flesh to eat, blood to drink (51-65): The idea that they need to receive His words and thereby receive Him (as it is related to eating our Lord's flesh and drinking His blood) has been dealt with before in Matthew 16:6-12. Even Jeremiah understood the idea of eating words as symbolically referring to taking in and receiving the words spoken (Jeremiah 15:16) and our Lord used this idea when He was tempted of the Devil: But he answered and said, It is written, Man shall not live by bread alone, but by every word that proceedeth out of the mouth of God. (Matthew 4:4)

One can only wonder at the bazaar doctrine of Transubstantiation.

CHAPTER 7

Jesus' Time in Galilee (vss. 1-9)

Jesus was exhorted to go up to Jerusalem to the Feast of Tabernacles, but chose to stay at Galilee. This He did because the Jews sought to kill Him and because He knew His time had not yet come.

- Jews sought to kill Him (1, 19, 25)
- His time had not yet come (6, 8, 30) cf. John 17:1

Jesus Goes Up to the Feast in Secret (vss. 10-13)

The feeling of the crowd is expressed in these passages. The Jews are there desiring Him (11); the crowd is there murmuring in division about Jesus, some saying, "He is a good man" while others say, "He deceives the people" (12). However, no man spoke openly for fear of the Jews (13).

Jesus in the Temple (vss. 14-39)

- Jesus taught doctrine in the temple and the crowd marveled at his teaching (14,15)
- Jesus assures them His doctrine is not His own (16 – 18)
- Jesus therefore teaches, just as Moses received from God circumcision and they perform it on the Sabbath day that the law be not broken, Jesus healed the lame man on the Sabbath, which He received of the Father and the law is not broken (19– 25)
- Now the crowd is beginning to know that it is Jesus speaking to them, and some believe (26– 31)
- The Pharisees hearing the people murmuring such things, send forth officers to take Him (32)
- Jesus foretells of His coming death and resurrection and the Jews confusion over it (33-36)
- Jesus' exhortation to believe on Him and they shall receive

living water (which is the Holy Ghost– vs 39) once He is
glorified (gone to the father– vss. 37-39, cf 17:1)

Division Among the People (vss. 40-44)
While there is a group professing that Jesus is the Christ
(vs. 41) their voice is drowned by the utter confusion of the
multitude. When Peter confesses that Jesus is the Christ, our
Lord will tell him that "flesh and blood hath not revealed
this unto him" i.e. this is not what was being commonly
reported by the multitude at that time (Matt. 16:17).

Division Among the Leaders (vss. 45-53)
The consternation over who Jesus is prevailed even to the
ones that should have known. They truly are the blind
leaders of the blind (Matt. 15:14).

CHAPTER 8

The Woman Caught in Adultery (vss. 1-11)

The historical account is self-explanatory. An interesting note is that according to Deuteronomy 22:22 both the man and the woman are to be dealt with, and since they stated they caught her in the "very act," it is suspicious that the man was not brought. Thus it is possible what our Lord wrote on the ground was Deuteronomy 22:22.

Revealing the heart of Israel's Religious leaders:
This chapter begins to unveil the religious leaders for who they are. Our Lord verbally removes their cloak of sin (John 15:22) to reveal their true nature. This chapter marks the beginning of the growing contention between Jesus Christ and the religious leaders. However, the Lord is in perfect control over the contention as seen by verse 59: Then took they up stones to cast at him: but Jesus hid himself, and went out of the temple, going through the midst of them, and so passed by.

Our Lord is letting the contention build to the point of boiling over at which time He will allow Himself to be crucified (John 17:1).

Contention Over the Father (vss. 12-59)

Knowing Not the Father (vss. 12-20)- Our Lord already dealt with this in chapter 5 in great detail. Since this contention is over the issue of the Father, He zeros in on this aspect, stating that it is His Father and Himself that bear witness: It is also written in your law, that the testimony of two men is true. I am one that bear witness of myself, and the Father that sent me beareth witness of me. (John 8:17-18)

Take careful note what our Lord states, "Ye neither know me nor my Father" (19 cf. 54,55). You need to understand the great significance of this. Later in this chapter our Lord tells them they are children of the Devil (44).

Knowing Not the Son (vss. 21-32)- Because they know not the Father, they know not the Son and therefore understand not His words (21-22,25, 43) and therefore do not believe on Him and as such will "die in your sins" (24). However, to the rebuke of the religious leaders, others do believe (30).

Two Fathers (vss. 33-46)- Our Lord now separates between His Father and their father: "I speak that which I have seen with my Father: and ye do that which ye have seen with your father." (John 8:38)

Our Lord moves through this chapter masterfully proving to these pride-filled religious men that they have a father, and he is not the Father in heaven. He says they know not the Father (19) and they know not the Son (25) and therefore they are not children of His Father (41). They do have a father (38, 41) and that father is the Devil (44).

Not of God (vss. 47-55)-Our Lord moves to the final conclusion, and this is the "nail in the coffin." As He has proved that they know not the Father and are therefore not His children, He further proves that they are not "of God." They are not begotten of God and are yet in their sins (24, 52).

Before Abraham was "I am" (vss. 56-59)- This chapter ends with the reality of the omnipresence of Jesus Christ; He is the great "I AM" of the Old Testament (Ex. 3:14). Abraham foreshadowed the sacrificial death of Jesus Christ when he offered up the ram in Isaac's stead, and as such he rejoiced to see the Lord's day. (Gen. 22:8, 13; Heb. 11)

CHAPTER 9

This chapter is a continuation of chapter 8: Then took they up stones to cast at him: but Jesus hid himself, and went out of the temple, going through the midst of them, and so passed by. (John 8:59)

And as Jesus passed by, he saw a man which was blind from his birth. (John 9:1)

Thus, in chapter nine we see Jesus still laying a frontal assault to the false religious system, for notice the miracle of healing the blind man is done on the Sabbath day (v.14). Our Lord is continuing to confront the religious leaders of the nation with the hypocrisy of their false religion, in an attempt to bring them to repentance. However, as we will see, they are going to "dig" in their heels, proving they are that hard-hearted and stiff-necked generation.

Healing of the Blind Man (vss. 1-3)
Notice that it was the disciples who first mentioned the issue of the blind man. They are under the impression that the man was in this state because of the sins of either himself or his parents (v.2). What they had been taught by their religious leaders regarding one born with infirmities was incorrect (Ezekiel 18:20); all sickness and disease comes from Adam and the fall of man (Rom. 5:12). And though man will reap the results of his sinful actions (Gal. 6:7,8), God was not judging this man "born blind" as a result of sin, but rather that the "works of God should be made manifest in him" (v. 3).

I Work the Work of Him That Sent Me (vs. 4)
By healing the blind man Jesus was performing the work

that God the Father had sent Him to do. This work was for the benefit of three groups of people in our text. The first group is the disciples. The disciples need to understand that the observance of the Sabbath is not to supersede mercy (see all of Matt. 12); Jesus did many other healings on the Sabbath (v. 14) for this very reason. The second group is made up of the religious leaders. The religious leaders needed to understand that they needed to take their place as sinners with the rest of mankind. They saw themselves as having no need of repentance of sins (v. 34, 41). They also needed to face the reality that this miracle took place at the hands of Jesus, and therefore He is the very Christ, the Son of God! The last group is the blind man himself and the blind leaders. In our text the blind man is set in direct contrast to the religious leaders. The blind leaders refuse to believe, while the man born blind does believe (vs. 35-37).

I Am the Light of the World (vs. 5)
By healing this blind man Jesus Christ is manifesting the truth that He is the Light of the World. The blind man will have light for the first time in his life. Spiritually, I saw for the first time in my life on April 14, 1994! How about you?

The Method of the Healing (vss. 6-7)
Jesus Christ chose not to heal various men and women in the same manner, lest we think that the clay had the healing properties in it, or lest we think that it was a method used, some incantation or spell. It was the very Son of God that healed this man!

Is Not This He That Sat and Begged? (vss. 8-12)
This man was known of all that came to the temple to worship, for he sat and begged, unable to provide for himself.

The Division Among the Pharisees (vss. 13-18)

The blind man is brought before the Pharisees who, upon questioning him, make the following statements that need to be considered, for they provide insight into how the religious leaders thought:

- This man is not of God because He keepeth not the Sabbath day. (v.15)
- How can a man that is a sinner do such miracles? (v.16)
- The blind man said he was a prophet but the scriptures state, "the Jews did not believe concerning Him." (v.18)

Questioning of the Parents (vss. 18-23)

The parents are brought into question and default to their Son out of fear: These words spake his parents, because they feared the Jews: for the Jews had agreed already, that if any man did confess that he was Christ, he should be put out of the synagogue. (John 9:22)

This once again is the reason they will remain "blind" in their ignorance; they chose not to believe that Jesus is the Christ, the Son of God (cf. 20:31).

Questioning of the Blind Man (vss. 24-34)

The questioning of the blind man starts with the statement from the Pharisees, "give God the praise: we know that this man is a sinner." No comment is necessary on this! The response to these religious, blind hypocrites is truly a beautiful thing! The man, who is not of the "religious elite," speaks to them with such clarity and boldness that it is clear he now "SEES." Notice the following:

- He answered them, I have told you already, and ye did not hear: wherefore would ye hear it again? will ye also be his disciples? (John 9:27)
- The man answered and said unto them, Why herein is

34

a marvellous thing, that ye know not from whence he is, and yet he hath opened mine eyes. (John 9:30)

• If this man were not of God, he could do nothing. (John 9:33)

These religious leaders are so committed in their stubborn resistance to Jesus being the Christ, they have rejected pure reason from a blind man. Notice their response to such reasoning arguments: They answered and said unto him, Thou wast altogether born in sins, and dost thou teach us? And they cast him out. (John 9:34)

The Belief of the Blind Man (vss. 35-37)

The bind man not only receives physical sight but receives spiritual sight as well, for he said, "Lord I believe." Now which one would you want to be, the man born blind spending his days from birth blind and begging, but understanding all the while that you are a sinner and in need of a Savior? Or would you rather be the Pharisee who lived sumptuously from day to day, enjoying the accolades of the crowd and the chief seats in the synagogue, and all the while being blind to your spiritual need?

Jesus and the Pharisees (vss. 39-41)

You see in this chapter there is more than one blind man. The Pharisees are blind to their spiritual condition, which is a state far worse than that of being physically blind.

CHAPTER 10

What the shepherds of Israel had become:
In John chapter ten our Lord deals with the leadership of the nation of Israel in a particular way. He puts forth the idea that they are miserable shepherds of Israel (in contrast to the good Shepherd) for they are nothing more than "hirelings" and "thieves and robbers;" "strangers" who care not for the sheep (10:13). However, Jesus Christ is not like them for He is the "good Shepherd" who giveth His life for the sheep (10:10-11).

The leadership of Israel being likened to miserable shepherds and the nation of Israel being likened to sheep is nothing new throughout the scriptures, but to fully appreciate this portion of scripture we need to read over Ezekiel 34.

The Shepherd of the Sheep (vss. 1-18)
• The parable of the shepherd and the sheep (1-5)
• They understood none of these things (6) (See John 8:43,47).
• Jesus is the Door (7,9). The sheepfold was an enclosure made of rocks with an opening for the door. The shepherd was to guard the herd at night by lying down across the opening, making himself the door.
• The shepherds of Israel are called "thieves and robbers" (1,10) (see Matt. 21:13).
• Jesus is the good Shepherd that will lay down His life for the sheep (15 cf. 17,18). Just as the shepherd lay across the door at night to protect the sheep, Jesus will lay down his life for the sheep.
• Other sheep (16): Once Israel is in her exalted position the Gentiles will be brought into the fold of God (Isa. 11:10).

Division Among the Jews (vss. 19-27)

The Jews demand of Him an answer of who He is, to which He responds that He has already told them but they believe Him not because they are not His sheep and hear not His voice (25-27).

I and My Father are One (vss. 28-31)

Okay then this is plain! However they don't believe and take up stones to stone Him! (31).

Many Good Works (vss. 32-42)

Once again our Lord exhorts them to believe His works. This chapter ends with the leaders of Israel not believing (39) while others "believed on Him" (42).

CHAPTER 11

The News of Lazarus (vss. 1-17)

He who thou lovest is sick (3): Notice first of all that Lazarus was merely sick when the messenger from Mary and Martha departs. Then after two more days (6) our Lord departs, arriving at Mary and Martha's house on the fourth day. Lazarus having been dead four days (16) means that the day the messenger arrived to tell of his sickness, Lazarus died.

Also notice that sickness does not mean that the Lord does not care for you; the Lord loved Lazarus: "he whom thou lovest is sick." Sickness is a part of the fall (Romans 8:22,23), and even death itself (Genesis 2:17, Hebrews 9:27). This body is in a state of decay. It is only temporal, for we are comforted with the reality that one day we will be clothed upon with a glorified body (2 Corinthians 5:1 cf. Philippians 3:21, 2 Peter 1:14). Our goal then is to glorify God, whether it be by life or death (See Phil. 1:20).

Lazarus sleepeth (11): For the redeemed, death is not the end, so for us the body is merely sleeping while the soul and spirit is present with the Lord (Dan. 12:2, Matt. 27:52,53; I Corinthians 15:51; II Corinthians 5:8; I Thess. 4:13,14).

The Arrival of Our Lord (vss. 18-33)

"I know he shall live again in the resurrection at the last day" (24): The resurrection has long been the hope of believers (Job 19:25,26, Dan. 12:2,3). Martha's belief (25-27) was as that of Peter (cf. Matthew 16:13-20).

The Raising of Lazarus (vss. 38-45)

The purpose of this miracle is stated throughout this text; it is so the people might believe on Him (notice 15,25-27,

42) which is the result (45), except for the leaders of Israel (47-48).

The Resistance from the Leadership of Israel (vss. 47-57)

As has been stated throughout our study in John, it is the leadership of the nation that is in total opposition to Christ (47, 48, 53, 57). Even when Caiaphas, the high priest, prophesied that Jesus should die for the nation and the people, they only sought the more to slay him (49-53).

CHAPTER 12

The final week...
Christ's final week is often referred to as the "passion week," and is the final week of our Lord's life upon the earth before His death, burial, and resurrection.

The Anointing of Jesus (vss. 1-8)
Mary's anointing is also recorded in Matt. 26:6-13 and Mark 14:3-9. Notice again that it is Martha who is "serving," true to her personality (Luke 10:38-40). The anointing was in view of the Lord's pending burial (vs. 7).

Judas voices his objection, not because he really cared for the poor, but rather because he "was a thief " (vs. 5,6). According to Matthew 26:14, it was following this event that Judas went to the chief priests to betray Christ.

The Crowd in Attendance (vss. 9-13)
These verses set the fervency of the spirit of the crowd at Jerusalem.
- Much people of the Jews — came not for Jesus sake only but also to see Lazarus who was raised from the dead (vs. 9), and proceed to take palm branches and shout Hosanna (vs. 12 cf. Zech. 9:9).
- The people that had been present at the raising of Lazarus from the grave are there, they saw the miracle (vss. 17,18).
- Chief Priest — consulting to put Lazarus to death also, for because of him many Jews believed (vss. 11-12); they are concerned for "behold the world is gone after him" (vs. 19).

• Certain Greeks also are there and desire to see Jesus (vs. 20).

All these groups add to the frenzy of the scene.

Prophecy Concerning His Entrance into Jerusalem (vss. 15-16)

This prophetic passage (Zech. 9:9) is concerning His first advent in contrast to His second (Rev. 19:11-13).

Prophecy Concerning His Death in Jerusalem (vss. 23-36)

In the following passages our Lord tells of His coming "glorification" when He will have died and ascended up to the Father (John 7:39, 12:23, 24, 28).

Prophecy Concerning Israel's Blindness (vss. 37-43)

Not only does this portion of scripture shoot down the deutero-Isaiah theory, but it also gives revealing insight into why Israel as a whole was blinded to their own Messiah. Two passages of Isaiah are quoted, and each deal with a certain aspect of how Israel perceived Jesus Christ.

Isaiah 53:1 deals with Israel perceiving Jesus Christ as a man smitten and afflicted of God, as an evildoer, not as a Savior dying for them. (See Isaiah 53:4,5)

Isaiah 6:9 deals with Israel's judicial blindness as a result of their continued rejection of light (Isaiah 6:9 cf. Romans 11:7-10).

The Union Between the Father and the Son (vss. 44-50)

Our Lord once again ties together the Father and the Son, and holds all who believe not the words of the Son accountable to God the Father (vs. 49,50).

CHAPTER 13

We've reached the point in Jesus' ministry that His witness to Israel is over. In the next four chapters (13-16) He will now turn to "His own" and prepare them for His departure from the world. He gives them instruction and comfort for the next phase of their ministry, the time when He will not be with them.

These chapters will end with chapter 17, our Lord praying for them before He, in chapter 18 is betrayed into the hands of sinners.

The Washing of the Disciples Feet (vss. 1-17)

As they finish supper our Lord proceeds to wash the disciples' feet. There is a great symbolic truth in what He is doing at this time that is more than just the mere act of washing their feet, for our Lord says:
What I do thou knowest not now; but thou shalt know hereafter. (John 13:7) (look at verse 12)

We need to look beyond the mere ceremonial washing to the great truth our Lord meant to convey. First off notice a few things about the context:
  - Jesus knew His hour had come, that He should depart from the world unto the Father. This is the context of this verse; He has His departure in view.
  - Having loved His own which were in the world, He loved them unto the end. Jesus is now focusing on "His own" in light of His departure, for He loved them!
  - The Supper. The disciples had just finished sitting at the table with our Lord. What a beautiful picture (Luke 22:30), the disciples sitting in an exalted position at our Lord's table.

— The Supper now being ended, the devil having now put into the heart of Judas Iscariot... The supper is ended and Jesus, knowing that the devil has now entered the heart of Judas, begins the final phase of His ministry.
— He riseth from the supper and laid aside His garments. Jesus now "ariseth" from the supper table and "laid aside His garments" and girds Himself with a towel.

The Symbolism Truth: In eternity-past Jesus spent time with the father in perfect fellowship with Him, but at the time appointed of the Father, He laid aside His glorious garments and took up a towel of humility (of flesh) and came to this earth, not as a king but as a servant.
— Our Lord now proceeds to go around the table and wash the disciples feet. He is there to serve them, He is there to care for them because He loves them, and He is there to lay down His life for them.
— So after He had washed their feet and had taken His garments and was sat down again... This is symbolic again of what He is going to do, He is come to lay down His life and return to the table with the Father (Heb. 10:12).
— Know ye what I have done to you? Again, they knew He had washed their feet, but there was something more to learn here. What they are to learn is what is to follow in this chapter and the ones preceding chapter 17.
— Ye aught to wash one another's feet.. The servant is not greater than his Lord. Here now is the lesson in the symbolism put forth in washing the disciples feet. They are to do as He has done. As He has loved them, they are to love one another; as He has served them, they are to serve one another; and as He will lay down His life for them, they will need to lay down their lives for one another: A new commandment I give unto you, That ye love one another; as I have loved you, that ye also

love one another. By this shall all men know that ye are my disciples, if ye have love one to another. (John 13:34-35) (See John 15:12 - 17)

This is the lesson, brought forth in the symbolic act of washing the disciples' feet. They will be further educated on this truth in the forthcoming chapters.

* It should also be noted Peter's brash words and our Lords response concerning washing the feet of the disciples (vss. 6-11). All were already washed (except one) by the washing of regeneration (Titus 3:5) but they need to have their feet washed because they have been walking around in the dust of the world (I John 1:9). This is reminiscent of the Laver in the Temple of which the priests had to continually wash their hands and feet (Ex. 30:18,19).

Judas Betrays the Son of Man (vss. 18-30)
These ominous verses are self-explanatory however it is noteworthy that they end with the word: He then having received the sop went immediately out: and it was night. (John 13:30)

A New Commandment (vss. 31-38)
The new commandment that was given when the Lord washed the disciples' feet is what they are to operate upon once the Lord is departed. They are to love one another, even to laying down their life for one another (See 1 John 3:11-16).

CHAPTER 14

Preparation for His Departure
As previously stated, our Lord in chapters 13 through 16 prepares His disciples for His departure back to the Father. For a little over three years He has taught and educated them on things concerning Himself and the long awaited kingdom and now in light of His departure being at hand and in light of troubling times ahead (verse 1) He gives them comfort and consolation.

The Comfort of a Home with the Father (vss. 1-6)
In my Father's house are many mansions: if it were not so, I would have told you. I go to prepare a place for you. And if I go and prepare a place for you, I will come again, and receive you unto myself; that where I am, there ye may be also. (John 14:2-3)

Our Lord's disciples are promised the very place that Abraham looked forward to (Hebrews 11:8-10 cf. Revelation 21). Jesus Christ is going to the Father and will come again and receive them unto Himself.

The Comfort of help in Time of Need (vss. 7-14)
And whatsoever ye shall ask in my name, that will I do, that the Father may be glorified in the Son. If ye shall ask any thing in my name, I will do it. (John 14:13-14)

What a great gift for these kingdom disciples! Peter himself is told whatever he binds on earth shall be bound in heaven (Matt. 16:19). And one need only to read the early portion of the book of Acts to see this great gift being utilized (Acts

3:1-9,19; 4:30; Acts 5:12-16). What a change from today where Paul himself prayed three times for his infirmity to be removed but was denied.

We have however the assurance that "all things work together for good to them that love God, to them who are the called according to his purpose. (Romans 8:28)

The Comfort of the Holy Ghost (vss. 15-26)
And I will pray the Father, and he shall give you another Comforter, that he may abide with you for ever; (John 14:16) This title allows great insight into one of the functions of the Holy Ghost; He is to be the Comforter. If someone is in need of comfort, it is reasoned they must be going through some form of sorrow, trouble or tribulation. This is exactly what is coming for the disciples (15:17-20; Matt. 24:8-10.)

Paul teaches us a great deal about the ministry of the Holy Spirit throughout his epistles but in 2 Corinthians chapter one specifically Paul educates us on the comforting aspect of the Holy Spirit (2 Corinthians 1:3-7). In this portion of scripture Paul teaches us two very important aspects to our comfort we receive of the Holy Ghost.

First, we are told the purpose of our comfort in all our tribulation is for the comforting of others. The second thing Paul teaches us is that the comfort we receive will be sufficient to the degree of the need; the comforting is not only sufficient but even supersedes the tribulation or sorrow.

The Comfort of Peace (vss. 27-31)
Peace I leave with you, my peace I give unto you: not as

the world giveth, give I unto you. Let not your heart be troubled, neither let it be afraid. (John 14:27) The disciples are promised peace, not as the world giveth! The world touts peace while the inner peace of the individual is at anything but peace!

We have the peace of God that keeps our hearts and minds:
And the peace of God, which passeth all understanding, shall keep your hearts and minds through Christ Jesus. (Philippians 4:7) Once you get saved you have peace with God, but you also have the peace of God! "come unto me and I will give thee rest".

Peter and the disciples were tossed about on the waves until our Lord commands, "peace be still" And he was in the hinder part of the ship, asleep on a pillow: and they awake him, and say unto him, Master, carest thou not that we perish? And he arose, and rebuked the wind, and said unto the sea, Peace, be still. And the wind ceased, and there was a great calm. (Mark 4:38-39)

CHAPTER 15

Vine and the Branches

Jesus Christ is the "true" vine and God the Father is the Husbandman that planted the vine (Jesus Christ) in His vineyard (Jerusalem). The branches are the disciples that are to partake of the vine and thereby bear much fruit. Fruit is what something produces, an apple tree bears its fruit, apples and so on. Fruit can be good or bad (Rom. 7:5). In this context it is a reference to bearing good fruit.

• The Fruitless branch (2): This branch is abiding in Christ (vine) however it is not producing fruit. Thus, growth in the Christian life is not automatic; it has to be cultivated! This is done through feeding on the nutrients of His Word (15:7). Paul says, "let the words of Christ dwell in you richly" (Col. 3:16). This is the reason for the attack on the Word of God, because it is vital to the Christian's growth! So it is the Word of God that works in the believer and begins to manifest Christ in his or her life, in speech, dress, choices we make and things we do or don't do. Fruit bearing is more than just soul winning, it is all areas of our Christian life that we yield to Him.

• The Fruitful branch (2): This branch is the fruitful Christian, one that is not only abiding in Christ but abounding in Christ! Now keep in mind two very important things regarding fruit bearing:
   1. Every fruit has a season (Psalms 1:1-4). The Christian needs to understand that there are seasons to the Christian life. Therefore God (husbandman) knows more than anyone not to expect fruit in the winter but rather at the harvest. Thus, Paul reminds us that at the judgment seat of Christ your life will only be considered as one big "work" (I Cor. 3:6-

15). Thus, you can probably expect to have seasons of fruitlessness, but it is not a life of fruitlessness!

2. For fruit to grow there needs to be a pruning process! To graduate from just bearing fruit to bearing much fruit the husbandman has to purge it (Look at verse 2)! The scriptures are filled with examples of this pruning process, it is the process of God bringing trials and tribulations in our lives to conform us into His image (12:6-8). Great chapter on this is 2 Corinthians 4!

• The branch that doesn't abide in Christ (6): There is no life apart from Jesus Christ! Notice it withers, and this is the life of everyone that is not in Christ, their life withers away and is accounted for nothing as far as eternity is concerned. Paul says prior to salvation ye are dead in trespasses and sins.

Commandment to Love (vss. 12,17)
The disciples are graduating from being merely servants to being friends, and as such they are going to be exhorted to "love one another" in light of the hate that the world will express (18). Paul tells us in Romans 13:8-10 that love is the fulfillment of the law, thus when we walk in love we obey the law of God (see: 5:1,2). But how can we do this? Can we do this in our sinful bodies? No, but the Holy Spirit will come, which is the Comforter, and He will give you the ability to glorify God in your members (26,27 cf. I Cor. 6:19,20).

CHAPTER 16

The Rise of Persecution (vss. 1-5)

The disciples are cautioned that those who seek to kill them think they do God's service. They have rejected the Son therefore they have rejected the Father (8:37-43), they know not the Father or Jesus Christ (3). The most notable person that will arise as the persecutor of the Jewish believers is Saul of Tarsus. At the stoning of Stephen one man stands above all the rest, Saul of Tarsus, the young man who held the clothes of Stephen's murderers (Acts 7:58-60; 8:1-3): Paul makes it clear he was of the sect of the Pharisees (Acts 23:6; Phil. 3:5) and zealous in this role. So relentless did Saul press the battle against Christ's followers and incite others to join that Saul received "authority and commission" from the chief priests to stamp out the worship of the Nazarene in "strange cities" and even as far away as Damascus compelling all who professed Christ to blaspheme (Acts 26:10-12). To the Galatians he writes how he persecuted the church beyond measure (Gal. 1:13). Ananias bears testimony to Saul's hatred for the Jerusalem saints: Then Ananias answered, Lord, I have heard by many of this man, how much evil he hath done to thy saints at Jerusalem: And here he hath authority from the chief priests to bind all that call on thy name. (Acts 9:13-14) Other martyrs will follow (Acts 12:2-3).

The Promise of the Holy Ghost (vss. 6-15)

In light of Jesus Christ leaving and ascending back to the Father the disciples are filled with "sorrow of heart" (6). But it is expedient that the Lord goes, for until He leaves the Comforter cannot come (7). The Comforter, when He comes, will have a ministry:

- To reprove the world of Sin (15:21-24), of righteousness (Rom. 1:16,17 vs. 10:1-8) and judgment to come (Acts

2:40).

- To guide them into all truth (thus He is called the Spirit of Truth vs.13)
- He will not speak of Himself (vs. 13)
- He will show things to come (vs. 13)
- He will glorify Christ (vs. 14)

The Departing of the Lord Back to the Father (vss. 16-33)

The Lord reminds the disciples He is departing to the Father. The disciples were confused on this issue for it was hid from them (Luke 9:44,45; 18:34), after the ascension of Jesus and the decent of the Holy Ghost they are bold to proclaim Christ and His resurrection (Acts. 2:14-40; 3:12-15; 4:8-14,31; 5:29-32).

CHAPTER 17

The Prayer of our Lord for the disciples: In chapters 13-16 you have the private ministry of our Lord to His disciples in the upper room. It ends with Jesus' prayer to the Father in all of John chapter 17. Our Lord prays for Himself and for His disciples.

Jesus Prays for Himself (vss. 1-5)

- Jesus knowing His "hour has come" prays to be glorified by the Father, that the Son may glorify Him (1).
- Jesus has glorified the Father while on earth (4). John 5:30 – "I seek not my own will but the will of the Father", 8:29 – "I do always those things that please Him" John 19:30 – "When Jesus therefore had received the vinegar, he said, It is finished: and he bowed his head, and gave up the ghost. "
- Jesus is desirous of the glory He had with the Father before the world was (5). Isaiah 42:8 declares that God the Father will not give His glory to another yet Jesus says He had the glory of the Father in eternity past, thus, Jesus Christ is God. (Philippians 2:5-11; John 1:1)

Jesus Prays for His disciples (vss. 6-19)

- Two key words are found in this next portion of scripture: world and the word.
- Jesus prays for the disciples that, though they are in the world they may not be of the world (14,15).
- Jesus gives them the answer to how they can be in the world but not of the world: Sanctify them through thy truth: thy word is truth (17). So as they go forth in the world (18) they are to stay in the word so they don't become of the world (19). When you are saved you get a spiritual washing (Titus 3:5). We that are the church are

sanctified, or set-apart to God, as we wash daily in God's Word (Ephesians 5:26). Thus we are not conformed to this world but transformed by the renewing of our minds (Romans 12:2.)

Jesus Prays for all who will believe on Him (vss. 20-26)

- As these disciples go out into the world and witness, others will come to believe, and those Jesus prays for as well. All our names can be seen here if you have believed on His name (20).
- Jesus prays that we all might be one (21), that the "world may believe." Now we are all one in Christ doctrinally (Galatians 3:28; Ephesians 4:4-6) however we are far from one practically; we are divided by denominational bounds of all kinds:

Now I beseech you, brethren, by the name of our Lord Jesus Christ, that ye all speak the same thing, and that there be no divisions among you; but that ye be perfectly joined together in the same mind and in the same judgment. (1 Corinthians 1:10)

For ye are yet carnal: for whereas there is among you envying, and strife, and divisions, are ye not carnal, and walk as men? (1 Corinthians 3:3)

For first of all, when ye come together in the church, I hear that there be divisions among you; and I partly believe it. (1 Corinthians 11:18)

- Thus, the church which is His body is not functioning as God intended (I Corinthians 12:12-25).

CHAPTER 18

The Arrest (vss. 1-14)

The Garden (1-2) – Where human history began it will end, in a garden. Adam disobeyed God in a garden and spun the whole human race into sin. But now the second Adam (1 Corinthians 15:45) will be betrayed in a garden to be handed over to sinful men and thereby provide the redemption for all the human race (See: Romans 5:12-21). Note also that in the place He is crucified there is a garden in which he will be buried (John 19:41-42).

Voice of Power (1-9) - This scene shows the depravity of man. After being knocked down by the mere voice of Jesus Christ, the men get back up and seek to take Him. Jesus is declaring for the second time that He is the great "I AM" (John 8:58). Note that our Lord will not back down in fear of man, but boldly proclaims "I AM He." Peter backed down in fear (vs. 17). Also notice it is the Lord who steps up and asks the question to Judas' mob, "Whom seek ye?"

The Cup (10-11) - Just earlier our Lord had prayed, "O my Father if it be possible let this cup pass from before me" (Matt.26:39). The cup symbolized the death of the cross He was about to encounter, the sins of the world that would be placed upon Him, and the separation from the Father. But this is His cup to drink; the world will drink of their own cup (Rev. 14:10, 16:19).

The Denial (12-27) - Jesus had predicted that Peter would deny Him three times (John 13:38). The three denials are listed in vss. 17, 25 and 27-28. The cock crowing was in the

3rd watch (evening: 6-9pm; midnight: 9-12; cock crowing: 12 midnight -3 am; morning: 3-6am—See Mark 13:35).

There is one event that is worth mentioning here, that is the look our Lord gave Peter upon his final denial. Our Lord is first led to Annas (13 cf. 24), then to Caiaphas (24). It was during this transportation that Peter was warming himself by the fire and our Lord looked over at him as he denied Him the third time (Luke 22:54-62).

The Rejection (vss. 28-40)
Judgment Hall (28) - Notice they would not go in the Judgment Hall lest they be defiled, but had no problem sentencing a man to death!

What is the Accusation? (29-32) - Pilate is not anxious to be involved in a Jewish court case especially around the Passover. If this person is causing problems for the Jews let them handle it (31). However, if the Jews had tried Him, His sentence would have been stoning; but God had declared that His Son would be crucified (John 3:14; 8:28; 12:32-33). Jesus was to bear the curse of the law, being made a curse for us; in order to do this He had to be hung on a tree (Duet. 21:22-23; Gal. 3:13).

Art thou King of Jews? - Jesus Christ in answering this question says, "now is my Kingdom not of this world," but it will be (Dan. 2:44). But "now," though born King, He will fulfill the role of Redeemer! Then He will go to receive of His Father a Kingdom, only to return as King of kings and Lord of lords (Rev. 19:16).

Not this Man but Barabbas—The Jews desire a robber and a murderer (Acts 3:14) in place of their Messiah. This is fitting, for our Lord had told them they are of their father the Devil; he was a murderer from the beginning. And now they not only commit the will of their father but also desire a murderer to be given them. (Look at John 8:44; Matt. 23:32,33).

CHAPTER 19

Christ Mocked (vss. 1-12)
Regarding Jesus Christ being King of the Jews, the soldiers planted a crown of thorns on His head, a purple and scarlet robe about Him and placed a reed in His hand. They bowed the knee before Him, mocking Him saying, "all hail King of the Jews" as they spit on Him and buffeted Him in the face, took the reed and smote Him on the head. (Matt. 27:26-31).
- He was scourged (1)
- He was slapped in the face before Annas (18:22)
- Spit on and beaten before Caiaphas (Matt. 26:67)
- And now He is scourged (1): the "stripes" by which ye are healed (Isaiah 53, I Pt. 2:24)
- Soldiers smote him with their hands (3)
- Crown of thorns (2) - redemption of a fallen creation (Gen. 3:17-19 cf. Rom. 8:22,23).
- I find no fault in Him (6) - this is the third time this statement is made (John 18:29, 38)
- He made Himself the Son of God (7) - This is why John wrote this epistle (20:31)
- Whence art thou? (9) - Pilate upon hearing the saying that Jesus made Himself the Son of God was the more "afraid" and then makes the statement, "Whence art thou?" showing He is beginning to wonder. Pilate would seek to let Him go but the Jews insisted if he let Jesus go that he is no friend of Caesar's (v. 12)

Christ, the King of the Jews (vss. 12-16)
Pilate delivers Jesus to be crucified.

Behold your King, we have no King but Caesar (vss. 14,15)
When men desire a king to rule over them they get a Barabbas.

When men desire God, they get liberty and freedom. Like Israel of old (I Samuel chapters 8, 12).

Christ Crucified (vss. 17-37)
And they crucified Him and two others with Him (18) - All you need to know about religion: The penitent thief, dies with sins in him, but not on him. Christ in the middle, dies with sins ON Him, but no sins IN Him. The unrepentant thief dies IN his sins, with his sins ON him. You either die with your sins on a Saviour who paid for them, or you die in your sins with your sins on you and pay for them yourself.
What I have written I have written (22) - God has written some books, and what He has written He has written, the book has the authority because of who wrote it (Rev. 20:12).
• It is Finished (30) - All the old testament sacrifices could not take away sin or cover them (Heb. 9:24-28). But Jesus Christ died once for all (I Pt. 2:24) and this now drives us in service for Him (2 Cor. 5:14,15). Jesus paid it all; all to Him I owe.
• Not a bone of Him was broken (36) - In fulfillment of Psalms 34:20 and in fulfillment of the Passover (Ex. 12:46).

Christ Buried (vss. 38-42)
Joseph of Arimathaea and Nicodemus take the body of Jesus, wrap it in linen cloths, and lay it in a new sepulcher. The next day the chief priests and Pharisees came to Pilate and desired him to place a guard outside the tomb (Matt. 27:62-66).

CHAPTER 20

The Resurrection is an essential part of the Gospel message (I Cor. 15:1-8) and a key doctrine to the Christian faith. It proves that Jesus Christ is the Son of God (Acts 2:32-36; Rom. 1:4) and that His atoning work on the cross has been completed (Rom. 4:24,25). The empty tomb is God's receipt, telling us that the debt has been paid. He is the Just and the Justifier (Rom. 3:26).

From the very outset the enemies of the Lord have sought to make the resurrection void :

- The Religious leaders claimed the body had been stolen (Matt. 28:11-15)
- The disciples could not have taken the body of Jesus, for it was guarded by Roman soldiers and sealed with a Roman seal (Mat. 27:62-66).
- The enemies of our Lord would not have taken the body; this would only prove the case for Jesus being the Christ.
- Perhaps the disciples had "visions" of the risen Lord, and they interpreted these as evidence for the revelation. But how could more than 500 people have the same testimony (I Cor. 15:6).
- Did the followers of our Lord go to the wrong tomb? Not likely, for they carefully watched where He was buried (Matt. 27:61, Mk. 15:47; Luke 23:55-57).

Thus, the resurrection is sure, Christ rose from the dead!

First to the Tomb, Mary Magdalene (vss. 1-18)

The first whom John names among those who came to Christ's sepulcher is Mary Magdalene. Mary Magdalene was the woman healed of seven devils (Mk. 16:9; Lk. 8:2). It was Mary Magdalene that: was at the cross (John 19:25) and was at the tomb at His burial (Matt. 27:60,61). And now we see Mary first to the tomb (John 20:1) (While it was "yet dark"), last to linger at the tomb, weeping (John 20:11) and first to see Him upon His resurrection (John 20:14-16). Through this we see the truth conveyed in Luke 7:27-50:

"Wherefore I say unto thee, Her sins, which are many, are forgiven; for she loved much: but to whom little is forgiven, the same loveth little." (Luke 7:47)

Think of all those who have a right estimation of themselves before God, those that understand the great debt forgiven them by grace through faith, and you will see a person with great zeal!

Paul was a shining example of this; Paul knew he was a sinner (I Tim. 1:15), and he understood he did not deserve to be called an apostle but by the grace of God (I Cor. 15:9,10).

Our Lord to the Disciples, "Peace be unto you..." (vss. 19-23)

Because of the cross work of Christ we have peace with God, and you can also have the peace of God (Ephesians 2:11-15).

Paul starts every one of his epistles with "grace" and "peace" unto you (Rom.1:7, I Cor. 1:3; 2 Cor. 1:2; Gal. 1:3; Eph. 1:2; Phil. 1:2; Col. 1:2 etc.)

Our Lord with Thomas; Believing Apart from Sight (vss. 24-31)

Thomas was not there when Jesus appeared unto them (vs. 24) so the disciples told him (vs. 25), but Thomas refused to believe them (vs. 25). Later our Lord did appear to him and he did believe (vss. 26-29).

It is in light of Thomas that John makes the statements in verses 29-31. We have not seen our Lord, but there are those who have and they have written down their testimony; do we believe it? (Cf. 2 Pt. 1:16-21) Then blessed are you!

CHAPTER 21

This final chapter of John is written to show the restoration of Peter as the leader of the other disciples, given his denial of the Lord earlier (John 18:17, 25,26-27). Peter is going to take the prominent place as head of the 12, as is seen in the early Acts period (Acts 2:14, 37-38; 3:12; 4:8; 5:3). It is Peter that states, "I go fishing" to which the others agree (vs.3), and it is Peter that our Lord asks three times "lovest thou me?" Thus, in this final chapter we see Peter learning valuable lessons.

Lesson on Fishing (vss. 1-14)
Peter announces "I go fishing" to which the other disciples agree (3). The emphasis is on Peter leading the disciples out fishing, and after fishing all night they caught nothing. The wording, "and that night they caught nothing" is stated in order for us to understand that Peter catching fish is not the purpose to which he is called. However, when our Lord appears to them on the shore and directs them to "Cast the net on the right side" they caught an abundance of fish. This is all to illustrate that Peter needs to get on the "right side" of the catching issue; our Lord had called the disciples to catch men, and Peter needs to lead them. Peter is called to be a fisher of men (read Luke 5:1-11).

Lesson on the Focus (vss. 15-17)
The Lord asks Peter three times, "lovest thou me?" (15,16,17) to which Peter replies in the affirmative. Now Jesus was not asking Peter these questions for His own benefit, for our Lord knew Peter's heart (John 2:25). But He asked this question three times for Peter's benefit. It was Peter that needed to be reminded of the one motivating factor in "feeding the sheep," and that is Peter's love for the Shepherd (I Pt. 2:25).

Lesson on Feeding (vss. 18-25)

Peter is also taught a lesson on feeding the sheep. Peter was told three times to feed the Lord's sheep (15,16,17). At that time the disciples had just finished a meal, therefore it is not physical food to which our Lord was referring. Peter is to be head of the 12, and as such he is to feed the flock of God! (I Peter 2:2; 5:1-4) There is also a great lesson for Pastors over the flocks to which God has called them; they are to feed the flock of God not with entertainment, but with the Word of God (I Tim. 1:3,10; 4:6,13,16; 5:17; 6:1,3; 2 Tim. 4:2,3).

Lesson on Following (18-25): Peter could not feed the sheep in his own strength; "they caught nothing." However, if Peter would "follow" the Lord he would always lead them to the right place (see the healing of the lame man Acts 3:1-16). When he followed his own way Peter -always found himself astray, but when following our Lord he found the will of God (I Pt. 4:1,2).

CONCLUSION

As we mentioned in the introduction, John's purpose in writing this gospel was to show forth that Jesus is the Christ, the Son of God (John 20:31). To this end John has succeeded. In chapter one He is the Word manifested, the light of the world. In chapter two He is the miracle worker at Cana. In chapter three He is the new birth to Nicodemus. In chapter four He is the water of life. In chapter five He is the healing waters of Bethesda. In chapter six He is the bread of life. In chapter seven He is the doctrine of God. In chapter eight He is the great "I AM" and in chapter nine He is sight to the blind. In chapter ten He is the Good Shepherd and the Door. In chapter eleven He is the Resurrection and the Life. In chapter twelve He is the King of Israel praised, and in chapter thirteen He is the King of Israel betrayed. In chapter fourteen He is the indwelling Holy Spirit of God. In chapter fifteen He is the Vine, and in chapter sixteen He is the Overcomer of the world. In chapter seventeen He is the Glory of God. In chapters eighteen and nineteen He is the King rejected, and in chapters twenty and twenty-one He is the Glorified Resurrected Lord of all the earth. Yes, the gospel of John is irrefutable proof that Jesus is the Christ, the very Son of God. And just in case one should doubt, John adds the following:

And there are also many other things which Jesus did, the which, if they should be written every one, I suppose that even the world itself could not contain the books that should be written. Amen. (John 21:25)

Appendix A
FURTHER STUDY NOTES

How the Gospels Portray Christ (Romans 15:8)
It is often questioned why four gospels. And it can be rightly said, to give a complete picture of Christ. However one fact is often over looked. The prophet Zechariah foretold that when the Messiah would come, He would be manifested in 4 distinct ways to the nation. The above references show this prophetic testimony.

- Matthew as King (Zech. 9:9)

- Mark as Servant (Zech. 3:8)

- Luke as the Son of Man (Zech. 6:12)

- John as God manifested in the Flesh (Zech. 13:7) - The man that is God's fellow is God's equal

The Purpose of John's Epistle
John emphatically states the purpose in writing his epistle: But these are written, that ye might believe that Jesus is the Christ, the Son of God; and that believing ye might have life through his name. (John 20:31)

The importance of believing that Jesus is the Christ the Son of God and thereby having life through His name is self evident. However this truth is far reaching even beyond our salvation.

Once the rapture of the church takes place, a remnant will be formed. A remnant of believers such as there was in the gospels, John being one of them. This future remnant will be accosted by false prophets claiming that Jesus was not the Christ and they need to look for another. For those who don't hold to Jesus being the Christ of God they will look for another to which role the antichrist assume.

Thus, this wonderful epistle for us, the body of Christ will also fulfill a very important doctrinal need for that yet future remnant.

Appendix B
OUTLINE OF JOHN'S GOSPEL

INTRODUCTION (1:1-14)

OPPORTUNITY (CHAPTERS 1:15-6)
He presents Himself to:
- His Disciples 1:19-2:12
- The Jews 2:13-3:36
- The Samaritans 4:1-54
- The Jewish leaders 5:1-47
- The multitude 6:1-71

OPPOSITION (CHAPTERS 7-12)
There is conflict with the Jewish leaders over:
- Moses 7:1-8:11
- Abraham 8:12-59
- Who Messiah is 9:1-10:42
- His miraculous power 11:1-12:36
- They would not believe on Him 12:37-50

OUTCOME (CHAPTERS 13-21)
- The faith of the disciples 13-17
- The unbelief of the Jews 18-19
- The victory of Christ 20-21

www.ingramcontent.com/pod-product-compliance
Lightning Source LLC
Chambersburg PA
CBHW060712030426
42337CB00017B/2842